From Zero to Podcast Overnight

By Edward Ellison

Copyright 2024 All Rights Reserved

Contents

Chapter 1 4
Chapter 2 10
Chapter 3 19
Chapter 4 28
Chapter 5 35
Chapter 6 44
Chapter 7 51
Chapter 8 60
Chapter 9 69
Chapter 10 77
Conclusion 84

Unlock the Secrets to Podcasting Success!

Are you ready to share your voice with the world and build a podcast that people can't stop listening to? Whether you're just starting out or looking to take your show to the next level, *Podcast Creators Guide To Success* is your ultimate guide.

Inside, you'll discover:
How to find your unique voice and purpose.

The essential tools and techniques to sound like a pro.

Strategies for branding, launching, and growing your audience.

Proven methods for monetizing without losing authenticity.

Tips for tracking your success and staying ahead of the curve.

From overcoming the fear of imperfection to navigating the future of podcasting, this step-by-step book has everything you need to create a podcast that stands out in today's competitive landscape.

Your audience is waiting—it's time to hit record. Start your podcasting journey today!

Chapter 1: Finding Your Podcast's Purpose

Podcasting has become one of the most dynamic platforms for sharing ideas, telling stories, and building communities. But with millions of podcasts available, the question isn't just about starting one—it's about creating a podcast that stands out and serves a clear purpose. The foundation of a successful podcast begins with defining its purpose and understanding its mission.

Choosing Your Podcast Topic

A podcast's topic is its heartbeat. It determines who will tune in and what they'll gain from listening. Selecting the right topic requires a balance of passion, expertise, and audience interest.

Identifying Your Passion and Expertise

Start by asking yourself: What excites you? What could you talk about endlessly without losing interest? Your passion will fuel your creativity and keep you motivated during the ups and downs of podcasting. But passion alone isn't enough; expertise also matters. List areas where you have knowledge, experience, or a unique perspective. This combination ensures your podcast is both engaging and credible.

For example, if you're passionate about cooking and have experience as a home chef, a podcast focused on easy, creative recipes could resonate with listeners. Alternatively, if you're a history enthusiast with a knack for storytelling, a podcast uncovering little-known historical events might be the perfect niche.

Researching Popular and Niche Topics

Once you've identified your interests and expertise, it's time to research the podcasting landscape. Use platforms like Apple Podcasts, Spotify, and Google Podcasts to explore popular categories and trending shows. Note the types of topics that perform well and identify gaps or underserved areas.

For instance, while true crime podcasts are immensely popular, there might be an opportunity to focus on unsolved cases from a specific region. Similarly, if you're exploring health and wellness, you could target niche audiences like busy parents or office workers seeking mindfulness techniques.

Look for these signs of a viable topic:

- Consistent listener demand.
- A community built around the subject.
- Opportunities for fresh or unique perspectives.

Defining Your Target Audience

Your audience is the cornerstone of your podcast's success. Who are you speaking to? Understanding your target listeners will help you tailor content to their needs and preferences.

Define your audience by answering these questions:

- **Demographics:** What is their age, gender, location, and education level?
- **Interests and Hobbies:** What are they passionate about or curious to learn?

- **Pain Points:** What challenges or problems do they face that your podcast could address?
- **Listening Habits:** When and how do they consume podcasts? Are they commuting, exercising, or relaxing at home?

For example, if you're creating a podcast on personal finance, your audience could range from young professionals managing student debt to parents saving for their children's education. The more specific your audience profile, the easier it is to craft episodes that resonate with them.

What's Your Unique Angle?

The podcasting world is crowded, but don't let that intimidate you. The key to standing out is finding a unique angle that sets your podcast apart.

Finding a Hook That Differentiates Your Podcast

Your "hook" is the distinctive element that makes listeners choose your podcast over others. It could be your storytelling style, your perspective, or the way you present information. Consider these strategies:

1. **Personal Experience:** Share your unique journey or perspective. For instance, if you've overcome a major life challenge, your podcast could inspire others navigating similar situations.
2. **Format Innovation:** Experiment with formats like serialized storytelling, live listener interactions, or a blend of interviews and solo episodes.

3. **Hyper-Specific Niches:** Narrow your focus to serve a dedicated audience. For example, instead of a general travel podcast, create one about budget travel for solo female travelers.

Examples of Unique Podcast Formats and Themes

Here are examples of podcasts that leverage unique angles:

- **The Daily Stoic:** Combines ancient philosophy with modern life advice, catering to a niche audience of philosophy enthusiasts.

- **Dr. Death:** A true crime podcast with a serialized, investigative format that unravels one chilling case over several episodes.

- **Song Exploder:** Focuses on deconstructing popular songs, offering a behind-the-scenes look at the creative process.

- **Call Me Candid:** A conversational podcast blending business advice with personal anecdotes for young entrepreneurs.

By innovating your approach, you create a podcast that attracts a loyal audience eager for your perspective.

Setting Goals for Your Podcast

A clear purpose and defined goals will guide your podcast's direction and measure its success. Whether your aim is to entertain, educate, influence, or monetize, your goals should align with your topic and audience.

Entertainment, Education, Influence, or Monetization?

1. **Entertainment:** If your primary goal is to entertain, focus on storytelling, humor, or drama. For example, comedy podcasts like *The Misfits Podcast* thrive on witty banter and relatable humor.

2. **Education:** Educational podcasts aim to inform and inspire. Shows like *TED Talks Daily* offer valuable insights across diverse topics, making them ideal for curious learners.

3. **Influence:** Some podcasts aim to build authority or foster social change. A fitness coach might create a podcast to establish expertise and attract clients, while an activist could use the platform to raise awareness for a cause.

4. **Monetization:** If income is your primary objective, focus on building an engaged audience that appeals to advertisers, sponsors, or premium content subscribers. For instance, a tech podcast could attract sponsorships from software companies.

Defining Success Metrics

Success looks different for every podcaster. Defining clear metrics helps track progress and stay motivated. Consider the following:

- **Downloads and Listens:** The number of times episodes are downloaded or streamed.

- **Audience Engagement:** Listener feedback, comments, and social media interactions.

- **Subscriber Growth:** The rate at which your audience expands over time.

- **Income:** Revenue from sponsorships, ads, merchandise, or premium content.
- **Impact:** Testimonials or stories from listeners who've benefited from your podcast.

Set realistic goals that align with your podcast's purpose. For example:

- In the first three months, aim for 500 downloads per episode.
- By the end of the first year, secure a sponsorship deal.
- Build a mailing list of 1,000 engaged subscribers within six months.

Final Thoughts

Defining your podcast's purpose isn't just the first step—it's the foundation for everything else. By choosing a topic you're passionate about, identifying your audience, finding your unique angle, and setting clear goals, you'll be on your way to creating a podcast that people want to listen to. Remember, the most successful podcasts aren't just about creating content—they're about building a connection with an audience eager to hear what you have to say.

Chapter 2: Planning the Perfect Podcast

Once you've found your podcast's purpose and identified your audience, it's time to plan the specifics. A well-thought-out plan not only makes the production process smoother but also ensures your podcast resonates with listeners. From deciding on the format to crafting a compelling identity, these steps will help you lay the foundation for a successful show.

Deciding on a Format

Your podcast's format is the structure that shapes each episode. It dictates how you deliver content, engage with listeners, and differentiate your show. Choosing the right format depends on your topic, skills, and preferences.

Solo, Co-Hosted, or Interview-Based?

1. **Solo Podcast**
    - **Pros:** Total control over content and scheduling. Great for building a personal brand and showcasing expertise.
    - **Cons:** Requires a lot of preparation and confidence to carry the show alone.
    - **Best For:** Experts, thought leaders, or storytellers who thrive on individual creativity.

   Example: A personal finance expert offering weekly tips and insights on managing money.

2. **Co-Hosted Podcast**

- **Pros:** Dynamic conversations, shared workload, and a natural chemistry that keeps listeners engaged.
- **Cons:** Requires consistent collaboration and scheduling with your co-host.
- **Best For:** Friends, colleagues, or professionals with complementary skills and interests.

Example: Two chefs discussing culinary trends, sharing recipes, and debating cooking techniques.

3. **Interview-Based Podcast**
   - **Pros:** Access to diverse perspectives and the potential to attract guests' audiences. Minimal preparation if guests provide the main content.
   - **Cons:** Requires effort to find and book interesting guests. Audio quality can vary depending on guest setups.
   - **Best For:** Those curious about other people's experiences or interested in showcasing industry leaders.

Example: A tech enthusiast interviewing startup founders about their journeys.

You can also blend formats, such as alternating between solo episodes and guest interviews. Experiment with different styles to discover what works best for you and your audience.

Episode Length and Frequency

Consistency is key when it comes to episode length and release schedules. Here's how to decide what works for your podcast:

- **Short Episodes (5-15 minutes):** Ideal for bite-sized tips, daily insights, or motivational content.
- **Medium Episodes (20-40 minutes):** The most common length for podcasts, perfect for casual listening during commutes or workouts.
- **Long Episodes (1 hour or more):** Suitable for in-depth interviews, storytelling, or panel discussions.

Match your episode length to your topic and audience's listening habits. For instance, a podcast about quick productivity hacks might work best with 10-minute episodes, while a true crime podcast could captivate listeners with hour-long episodes.

Determine your release frequency based on your capacity and audience expectations:

- **Daily:** Best for news or short, consistent content.
- **Weekly:** The most common schedule, balancing consistency with manageable workload.
- **Biweekly or Monthly:** Suitable for highly produced shows or hosts with limited time.

Stick to a consistent schedule to build trust with your audience.

Structuring Episodes for Maximum Engagement

An engaging structure keeps listeners hooked from start to finish. A typical podcast episode might follow this format:

1. **Introduction (1-2 minutes):**
   - Briefly welcome listeners and set the tone for the episode.
   - Tease the main topic to build anticipation.
2. **Main Content (10-40 minutes):**
   - Present the core discussion, interview, or story.
   - Use clear segments or transitions to maintain flow.
3. **Call to Action (1-2 minutes):**
   - Encourage listeners to subscribe, leave a review, or follow on social media.
   - Mention any resources, links, or upcoming episodes.
4. **Closing (1-2 minutes):**
   - End with a memorable sign-off, such as a tagline or catchphrase.

Add variety with segments like Q&A sessions, listener shoutouts, or rapid-fire questions for guests. Consistency in structure helps listeners know what to expect, while occasional surprises keep them engaged.

Naming Your Podcast

Your podcast's name is often the first thing potential listeners notice. It should be memorable, descriptive, and aligned with your brand.

Tips for Choosing a Memorable, Descriptive, and Brandable Name

1. **Be Clear and Concise:**
   - Choose a name that clearly conveys your podcast's theme or purpose.
   - Avoid overly complex or ambiguous names.

Example: *The History Buff* instantly tells listeners it's a podcast for history enthusiasts.

2. **Incorporate Keywords:**
   - Use words related to your topic to improve searchability.
   - For instance, a podcast about plant care might include "Garden" or "Botany" in the name.

3. **Add a Creative Twist:**
   - Play with puns, alliteration, or cultural references to make your name stand out.

Example: *Crime and Wine,* a true crime podcast where hosts discuss cases over a glass of wine.

4. **Ensure Longevity:**
   - Avoid trends or slang that might become outdated.
   - Choose a name that accommodates future growth or topic expansions.

Checking for Name Availability

Before finalizing your name, ensure it's unique and available across platforms:

1. **Podcast Directories:** Search platforms like Apple Podcasts and Spotify to check for existing podcasts with similar names.

2. **Domain Names:** Use tools like Namecheap or GoDaddy to find and secure a matching website domain.

3. **Social Media Handles:** Check availability on platforms like Instagram, Twitter, and Facebook to maintain consistent branding.

4. **Trademarks:** Conduct a trademark search to avoid potential legal issues.

Securing consistent branding across platforms makes it easier for listeners to find and follow your podcast.

Crafting Your Podcast Identity

A strong podcast identity sets the tone for your show and helps it stand out visually and descriptively.

Designing Eye-Catching Podcast Cover Art

Podcast cover art is your visual calling card. It appears in directories, social media posts, and promotional materials. Here's how to make it stand out:

1. **Follow Platform Guidelines:**
    - Create a square image (minimum 3000 x 3000 pixels).

- Use a high-resolution format for clarity across devices.

2. **Keep It Simple:**
    - Avoid cluttered designs. Focus on a clear focal point, such as the podcast name or an iconic image.

3. **Use Bold, Readable Fonts:**
    - Ensure your title is legible even at thumbnail size.

4. **Choose a Color Scheme:**
    - Select colors that reflect your podcast's tone and personality. For example, vibrant colors for a comedy show or muted tones for a serious podcast.

5. **Include Your Logo or Portrait (Optional):**
    - Incorporate a personal touch, such as your photo or a recognizable logo, if it aligns with your brand.

Tools like Canva, Adobe Spark, or Photoshop can help you design professional-looking cover art even without graphic design experience. If you prefer, hire a freelance designer through platforms like Fiverr or 99designs.

Writing an Engaging Podcast Description

Your podcast description is your elevator pitch. It's what potential listeners read when deciding whether to hit play. Craft a description that highlights your podcast's value and appeals to your target audience:

1. **Start with a Hook:**
    - Begin with a compelling question or statement that grabs attention.

Example: "Do you ever wonder what it's like to step into the shoes of a startup founder? Discover the highs, lows, and everything in between on *Startup Stories*."

2. **Explain the Value:**
    - Clearly state what listeners will gain from your podcast. Is it entertainment, education, or inspiration?

Example: "Each week, we bring you actionable tips and expert insights to help you build your dream business."

3. **Mention Your Unique Angle:**
    - Highlight what sets your podcast apart from others in the same niche.

Example: "Unlike other business podcasts, we focus on candid, unfiltered conversations with industry leaders."

4. **Include Keywords:**
    - Incorporate relevant keywords to improve searchability in podcast directories.

5. **Add a Call to Action:**
    - Encourage listeners to subscribe, follow, or leave a review.

Example: "Hit subscribe and join our community of aspiring entrepreneurs today!"

Keep your description concise (2-3 paragraphs) and update it periodically to reflect new developments or milestones.

Final Thoughts

Planning the perfect podcast involves careful consideration of format, structure, and identity. By choosing the right format, naming your podcast strategically, and crafting a strong visual and descriptive brand, you'll create a solid foundation for your show. These elements not only attract listeners but also ensure they keep coming back for more.

Chapter 3: Essential Tools and Tech for Beginners

Launching a podcast doesn't require a professional studio or a massive budget, but investing in the right tools and technology is critical to producing quality content that keeps listeners engaged. This chapter covers everything from recording equipment basics to software options and podcast hosting platforms, providing you with a comprehensive guide to get started.

Recording Equipment Basics

High-quality audio is the cornerstone of a great podcast. While content matters most, poor sound quality can drive listeners away, so it's important to choose the right equipment for your setup.

Recommendations for Microphones

The microphone is arguably the most important piece of equipment for any podcaster. Here are three main types to consider:

1. **USB Microphones**
    - Ideal for beginners due to their plug-and-play simplicity.
    - Connect directly to your computer without the need for additional equipment.
    - Examples:
        - **Blue Yeti**: A versatile and popular choice offering multiple recording patterns.

- **Audio-Technica ATR2100x**: Known for its excellent sound quality and durability.

2. **XLR Microphones**
   - Preferred by more advanced podcasters for superior audio quality.
   - Require an audio interface or mixer to connect to your computer.
   - Examples:
     - **Shure SM7B**: A professional-grade microphone with exceptional clarity.
     - **Rode Procaster**: Designed specifically for broadcasting and podcasting.

3. **Lavalier Microphones**
   - Small clip-on microphones, great for mobile or video-based podcasts.
   - Examples:
     - **Rode SmartLav+**: Affordable and compatible with smartphones.
     - **Sennheiser ME 2-II**: High-quality audio in a compact design.

Recommendations for Headphones

Monitoring your audio while recording and editing is essential to ensure quality. Look for closed-back headphones to block external noise:

- **Budget-Friendly:** Audio-Technica ATH-M20x or Sony MDR-7506.
- **Premium:** Beyerdynamic DT 770 Pro or Sennheiser HD 280 Pro.

Pop Filters and Boom Arms

- **Pop Filters:** These reduce plosive sounds (like "p" and "b") for cleaner audio. Options like the Aokeo Pop Filter or Neewer Professional Pop Filter are affordable and effective.
- **Boom Arms:** These hold your microphone in place, providing flexibility and reducing desk noise. Popular options include the Rode PSA1 or Heil Sound PL-2T.

Budget-Friendly and Premium Setups

1. **Budget Setup (Under $150):**
    - Microphone: Audio-Technica ATR2100x ($100)
    - Headphones: Audio-Technica ATH-M20x ($50)
    - Pop Filter: Aokeo Pop Filter ($10)

2. **Premium Setup ($500+):**
    - Microphone: Shure SM7B ($400)
    - Audio Interface: Focusrite Scarlett 2i2 ($170)
    - Headphones: Beyerdynamic DT 770 Pro ($150)

- Boom Arm: Rode PSA1 ($100)

Recording Software Options

Choosing the right recording software depends on your experience level, budget, and specific needs. Fortunately, there are excellent options for both beginners and professionals.

Free Software

1. **Audacity**
    - Open-source and widely used.
    - Features include multi-track editing, noise reduction, and effects.
    - Ideal for beginners on a budget.

2. **GarageBand** (Mac Only)
    - User-friendly with built-in features for recording and editing.
    - Includes loops and sound effects for enhancing episodes.

Paid Software

1. **Adobe Audition**
    - Industry-standard software with advanced editing capabilities.
    - Monthly subscription required ($20.99/month).

- Ideal for podcasters seeking professional-level tools.

2. **Hindenburg Journalist**
    - Designed specifically for podcasters and journalists.
    - Features include automatic sound leveling and intuitive editing.
    - One-time purchase ($95+).

3. **Logic Pro X** (Mac Only)
    - Advanced software for professional-level editing.
    - Includes features like EQ adjustments and multi-track mixing.

Tips for Ensuring Clean Audio Quality

- **Record in a Quiet Environment:** Minimize background noise by recording in a small, enclosed space. Use blankets or foam panels to reduce echo.
- **Monitor Audio Levels:** Aim for levels between -12dB and -6dB to avoid distortion.
- **Use Noise Reduction Tools:** Most software includes features to eliminate background hum or hiss.
- **Perform Test Runs:** Always test your setup before recording an episode.

Hosting Platforms and Distribution

Once you've recorded and edited your episodes, you'll need a hosting platform to store and distribute your podcast. Hosting platforms act as a central hub, providing your podcast's RSS feed to directories like Spotify and Apple Podcasts.

What is a Podcast Hosting Platform?

A podcast hosting platform is a service that:

- Stores your audio files.
- Generates an RSS feed for distribution.
- Tracks analytics such as downloads and listener demographics.

Without a hosting platform, it's impossible to share your podcast on major directories.

Overview of Hosting Platforms

1. **Buzzsprout**
    - User-friendly with detailed analytics.
    - Free plan available (limited hours) and affordable paid plans starting at $12/month.
    - Additional features include transcription and dynamic content insertion.

2. **Anchor (by Spotify)**
    - 100% free with unlimited hosting.
    - Simple interface for beginners.
    - Integrated monetization options, such as ad sponsorships.

3. **Libsyn**
    - One of the oldest and most reliable platforms.
    - Plans start at $5/month.
    - Robust analytics and advanced features for experienced podcasters.

4. **Podbean**
    - Comprehensive hosting and monetization options.
    - Paid plans start at $9/month.
    - Offers a user-friendly app for mobile recording and publishing.

5. **Transistor**
    - Focused on professional podcasters and businesses.
    - Includes unlimited podcasts under one account.
    - Plans start at $19/month.

Setting Up Distribution

After choosing a hosting platform, it's time to distribute your podcast to major directories. Here's a step-by-step guide:

1. **Submit to Spotify**

- Most hosting platforms automatically distribute to Spotify. If not, submit your RSS feed through Spotify for Podcasters.

2. **Submit to Apple Podcasts**

    - Create an Apple ID and sign in to Apple Podcasts Connect.
    - Submit your RSS feed and wait for approval (typically 24-72 hours).

3. **Submit to Google Podcasts**

    - Use Google Podcasts Manager to add your RSS feed.
    - Verify ownership of your podcast and publish.

4. **Explore Other Directories**

    - Distribute to platforms like Amazon Music, Stitcher, and TuneIn for additional reach.

Tips for a Successful Launch

- **Publish Multiple Episodes:** Release 2-3 episodes at launch to give listeners a reason to subscribe.

- **Optimize Metadata:** Use relevant keywords in your podcast title, description, and episode titles to improve discoverability.

- **Promote on Social Media:** Share teaser clips, behind-the-scenes content, and episode updates.

Final Thoughts

Investing in the right tools and technology doesn't have to be overwhelming or expensive. Start with the basics, upgrade as you grow, and focus on creating high-quality content. With the right equipment, software, and hosting platform, you'll be well on your way to launching a podcast that stands out in a competitive landscape.

Chapter 4: Creating Engaging Content

A podcast's success hinges on its ability to capture and hold an audience's attention. No matter your topic, creating engaging content requires thought, preparation, and a touch of creativity. In this chapter, we'll dive into storytelling, episode planning, and strategies to keep your listeners coming back for more.

The Art of Storytelling

Storytelling is a powerful tool that turns ordinary content into something memorable and compelling. Whether you're sharing a personal experience, explaining a concept, or conducting an interview, a strong narrative structure can make all the difference.

Structuring Your Episodes for Impact

Every great story—and podcast episode—has a clear structure. Following a well-defined format keeps your audience engaged and ensures your message resonates. Here's a common structure to consider:

1. **The Hook**
    - Grab the listener's attention within the first 30 seconds.
    - Start with an intriguing question, surprising fact, or emotional anecdote.
    - Example: "Did you know that 90% of people give up on their New Year's

resolutions by February? Today, we're exploring how to stay on track."

2. **The Middle (Core Content)**
    - Dive into the main topic or story. Break it into digestible segments to maintain interest.
    - Use examples, data, or expert insights to support your points.
    - Keep transitions smooth to avoid losing momentum.

3. **The Conclusion**
    - Recap the key takeaways or highlights from the episode.
    - End with a call to action, such as encouraging listeners to subscribe, share, or try something new based on your episode.
    - Example: "Remember, small daily habits lead to big changes. Start today and watch the transformation unfold."

Adding Personal Anecdotes and Relatable Elements

Sharing personal stories or relatable experiences can create a stronger connection with your audience. People are drawn to authenticity, so don't be afraid to let your personality shine.

- **Use Vulnerability:** Share challenges you've faced or lessons you've learned to make your content more relatable.

- Example: In a podcast about entrepreneurship, you might share a story about a failed business venture and what it taught you.
- **Connect to Universal Themes:** Focus on emotions and situations most listeners can relate to, such as love, fear, ambition, or failure.
- **Incorporate Listener Stories:** Invite your audience to share their experiences and weave them into your episodes.

Planning and Scripting Your Episodes

Even the most engaging content requires preparation. Proper planning ensures your episodes flow smoothly and deliver value to your audience.

Striking the Balance Between Scripting and Improvisation

One of the biggest challenges podcasters face is deciding how much to script. Over-scripting can make your delivery sound robotic, while improvising too much can lead to rambling. Here's how to strike the right balance:

1. **Fully Scripted:**
   - Ideal for storytelling or educational podcasts where precision is crucial.
   - Write your script in a conversational tone to avoid sounding stiff.
2. **Bullet Points:**

- Create an outline with key points, examples, and transitions.
- Allows for natural delivery while keeping you on track.

3. **Freeform with Preparation:**
   - Research your topic thoroughly and rehearse the flow of your episode.
   - Works well for experienced podcasters who thrive on spontaneity.

Creating an Episode Template or Checklist

An episode template streamlines your production process and ensures consistency. Here's an example template to follow:

1. **Episode Title:** Craft a title that's clear, descriptive, and enticing.
2. **Introduction:** Write a brief opening to set the tone and introduce the topic.
3. **Main Points:** Outline the core content and supporting examples.
4. **Transitions:** Plan how you'll move from one segment to the next.
5. **Call to Action:** Include a specific request, such as subscribing or visiting your website.
6. **Closing:** End with a memorable sign-off, such as a tagline or gratitude message.

Engaging Your Audience

Engagement is about more than just delivering great content; it's about creating a two-way relationship with your listeners. Here are some strategies to make your podcast interactive and captivating.

Tips for Asking Compelling Questions (if Interviews Are Involved)

Interviews can be a fantastic way to bring fresh perspectives to your podcast. The key is asking questions that spark interesting conversations. Follow these tips:

1. **Do Your Research:**
    - Learn about your guest's background, expertise, and recent work.
    - Reference specific achievements or topics to show you're prepared.

2. **Ask Open-Ended Questions:**
    - Avoid yes/no questions. Instead, encourage your guest to elaborate.
    - Example: Instead of asking, "Do you enjoy writing?" ask, "What inspired you to become a writer?"

3. **Dig Deeper:**
    - Follow up on interesting points with deeper questions.
    - Example: "You mentioned X was a turning point. Can you share more about what made it so impactful?"

4. **Keep It Conversational:**
    - Allow the conversation to flow naturally while guiding it back to your main topic when necessary.

Using Humor, Pacing, and Tone Effectively

Your delivery plays a significant role in keeping listeners engaged. Consider these tips:

1. **Humor:**
    - Use humor to lighten the mood and make your podcast more enjoyable.
    - Avoid forced jokes or humor that could alienate your audience.

2. **Pacing:**
    - Vary your pacing to maintain interest. Speak slower during reflective moments and faster during exciting points.
    - Avoid monotone delivery by emphasizing key words and phrases.

3. **Tone:**
    - Match your tone to your podcast's theme. For example, a motivational podcast should sound uplifting, while a true crime podcast might use a more serious tone.

Encouraging Listener Interaction

Engaging your audience directly builds loyalty and fosters a sense of community. Here's how to involve your listeners:

- **Social Media Engagement:** Create polls, ask questions, and share behind-the-scenes content on platforms like Instagram or Twitter.
- **Listener Questions:** Invite listeners to submit questions or topic ideas for future episodes.
- **Callouts:** Give shoutouts to listeners who leave reviews, share your podcast, or contribute to discussions.
- **Contests and Giveaways:** Offer incentives for audience participation, such as free merchandise or exclusive content.

Final Thoughts

Creating engaging content is both an art and a science. By mastering storytelling, planning your episodes thoughtfully, and actively involving your audience, you can craft a podcast that not only informs but also inspires and entertains. Remember, the best podcasts are those that create a meaningful connection with their listeners.

Chapter 5: Recording and Editing Like a Pro

Recording and editing are where your podcast truly comes to life. High-quality audio is essential to retaining listeners and maintaining a professional image. Fortunately, achieving great sound doesn't require a professional studio or years of experience—just the right techniques, tools, and attention to detail. In this chapter, we'll explore how to set up your recording space, master recording best practices, and polish your episodes through effective editing.

Setting Up Your Recording Space

Your recording environment has a significant impact on audio quality. A well-prepared space can minimize distractions and produce clean, professional sound.

Tips for Soundproofing and Creating a Quiet Environment

1. **Choose the Right Location:**
    - Select a quiet room away from high-traffic areas, windows, and appliances.
    - Avoid rooms with hard surfaces that can reflect sound, such as kitchens or tiled bathrooms.

2. **Reduce Echo:**
    - Use soft furnishings like rugs, curtains, and cushions to absorb sound.
    - Place a blanket or quilt over hard surfaces to minimize reflections.

- For a budget-friendly solution, record inside a closet surrounded by hanging clothes.

3. **Block External Noise:**
   - Close doors and windows to reduce outside sounds like traffic or birds.
   - Use draft stoppers or weather stripping to seal gaps around doors.
   - Turn off noisy appliances like fans, air conditioners, or refrigerators during recording.

4. **Add Acoustic Panels:**
   - Install foam panels or bass traps to absorb sound and prevent echoes.
   - For a DIY option, hang thick blankets or sound-absorbing curtains on walls.

5. **Control Microphone Proximity:**
   - Keep your microphone close to your mouth to reduce room noise pickup.
   - Use a directional microphone to focus on your voice while ignoring background sounds.

Avoiding Common Pitfalls Like Echo and Background Noise

- **Avoid Large, Open Spaces:**

- o Recording in a large, empty room can create reverb. Stick to smaller spaces with soft furnishings.
- **Check for Hum and Buzz:**
  - o Test your recording setup for electrical hums or interference from devices like computers or fluorescent lights.
- **Use a Pop Filter:**
  - o A pop filter placed in front of your microphone reduces harsh plosive sounds (e.g., "p" and "b" sounds).

Recording Best Practices

Once your recording space is ready, focus on techniques that ensure clear and consistent audio quality.

Microphone Techniques for Clear Audio

1. **Maintain Proper Distance:**
   - o Keep your mouth 6-12 inches from the microphone.
   - o Experiment with positioning to find the sweet spot for your voice.
2. **Speak at a Consistent Volume:**
   - o Avoid moving closer or farther from the microphone while speaking.
   - o Use a microphone with a cardioid pattern to minimize off-axis sounds.

3. **Use a Pop Filter and Shock Mount:**
    - A pop filter reduces plosive sounds, while a shock mount minimizes vibrations from desk movements.
4. **Record in Segments:**
    - Break your episode into smaller sections to make re-recording easier if needed.
5. **Warm Up Your Voice:**
    - Do vocal exercises or read a few sentences aloud before recording to improve clarity and tone.

Monitoring Levels During Recording

1. **Set Appropriate Gain Levels:**
    - Adjust the gain on your microphone or audio interface so your voice peaks between -12dB and -6dB. This prevents distortion while leaving room for post-production adjustments.
2. **Use Headphones for Monitoring:**
    - Wear closed-back headphones to hear your voice and detect issues like background noise or clipping in real-time.
3. **Test Before Recording:**
    - Record a short sample and listen back to ensure the levels, clarity, and tone are balanced.

4. **Avoid Clipping:**
    - Clipping occurs when your audio peaks exceed 0dB, resulting in distortion. Keep an eye on your levels to avoid this.

Editing Basics

Editing is where you refine your recording into a polished, professional episode. A good edit removes distractions, enhances clarity, and creates a seamless listening experience.

Cutting Out Filler Words and Awkward Pauses

1. **Identify Problem Areas:**
    - Listen for filler words like "uh," "um," "like," and "you know."
    - Remove long pauses or repetitive phrases that disrupt the flow.

2. **Keep It Natural:**
    - Avoid over-editing, which can make the conversation sound robotic.
    - Leave occasional filler words if they contribute to a conversational tone.

3. **Use Editing Tools:**
    - Most editing software includes tools for cutting, splicing, and trimming audio.
    - Use shortcuts to speed up the editing process.

Adding Intros, Outros, and Music

1. **Craft a Memorable Intro:**
   - Include a brief introduction to your podcast and a teaser for the episode.
   - Example: "Welcome to The Creative Chronicles, where we explore the secrets of successful creators. Today, we're diving into the world of storytelling."

2. **Include a Strong Outro:**
   - Thank your listeners and encourage them to take action, such as subscribing, leaving a review, or visiting your website.
   - Example: "Thanks for tuning in! Don't forget to follow us on Instagram and share this episode with a friend."

3. **Select Appropriate Music:**
   - Use royalty-free music for your intro, outro, or transitions.
   - Keep music volume low to avoid overpowering your voice.

Tools for Polishing Audio Quality

1. **Noise Reduction:**
   - Use noise reduction tools to remove background hum or hiss. For example, Audacity offers a "Noise Reduction" effect.

2. **Equalization (EQ):**

- Adjust EQ settings to balance frequencies. Enhance clarity by reducing bass and boosting midrange frequencies for vocals.

3. **Compression:**
    - Apply compression to even out volume levels and make your audio sound more professional.

4. **Normalization:**
    - Normalize your audio to ensure consistent volume levels throughout the episode.

5. **Plugins and Effects:**
    - Experiment with plugins like de-essers (to reduce harsh "s" sounds) and limiters (to prevent clipping).

Step-by-Step Editing Process

1. **Import Your Audio:**
    - Load your recording into your editing software.
    - Arrange files in separate tracks for the host, guest, and background music.

2. **Trim Unnecessary Sections:**
    - Remove pre-recording chatter, long pauses, or off-topic tangents.

3. **Apply Noise Reduction and EQ:**

- Use noise reduction to clean up background noise, then adjust EQ for vocal clarity.

4. **Cut Filler Words and Awkward Pauses:**
    - Edit out excessive "um" or "uh" sounds, but leave natural conversational pauses.

5. **Add Intros, Outros, and Music:**
    - Insert your podcast's intro and outro music.
    - Use fade-in and fade-out effects for smooth transitions.

6. **Apply Compression and Normalize:**
    - Use compression to balance audio levels and normalization to ensure consistency.

7. **Listen and Review:**
    - Play through the entire episode to catch any missed edits or audio issues.

8. **Export the Final File:**
    - Export your audio in a high-quality format, such as MP3 (192-320 kbps) or WAV.

Final Thoughts

Recording and editing your podcast like a pro takes practice, but with the right techniques and tools, you can produce episodes that sound polished and professional. Focus on creating a clean recording environment, mastering microphone techniques, and refining your editing skills. The effort you put into this stage will shine through in the final product, helping you stand out in a competitive podcasting landscape.

Chapter 6: Branding and Launching Your Podcast

Branding and launching your podcast is a crucial phase where you set the tone for your show, attract your audience, and make a strong first impression. This chapter will guide you through creating a strong brand identity and developing a launch strategy that ensures your podcast starts with a bang.

Creating a Strong Brand Identity

Your podcast's brand identity goes beyond its name or logo. It encompasses the visuals, tone, and messaging that make your podcast recognizable and memorable. A consistent and compelling brand helps you connect with your audience and build loyalty over time.

Consistent Visuals, Tone, and Messaging

1. **Visual Identity**

    - **Podcast Cover Art:** This is the first thing potential listeners will see, so it needs to be eye-catching and professional. Use bold colors, clear typography, and minimal clutter. Ensure your cover art meets the standard size requirements (3000 x 3000 pixels).
    - **Logo and Fonts:** Choose a logo and fonts that reflect your podcast's theme and tone. For instance, a true crime podcast might use dark colors and bold fonts, while a comedy

podcast might lean towards vibrant colors and playful fonts.

- **Social Media Graphics:** Maintain a consistent aesthetic across platforms. Use similar colors, filters, and templates for your posts.

2. **Tone and Voice**

- **Define Your Personality:** Is your podcast formal and informative, casual and conversational, or humorous and lighthearted? Your tone should reflect your audience's expectations.
- **Consistent Language:** Use the same language style across episodes, social media posts, and other communications to create a cohesive brand.

3. **Messaging**

- **Tagline:** Create a tagline that encapsulates your podcast's purpose. For example, a fitness podcast might use, "Helping You Build a Healthier Life One Episode at a Time."
- **Mission Statement:** Define your podcast's goals and what listeners can expect to gain.

Crafting a Compelling Intro and Outro

Your podcast's intro and outro are essential for establishing your brand and leaving a lasting impression.

1. **Podcast Intro**

- **Grab Attention:** Start with a hook that captivates listeners within the first 10 seconds.
- **Introduce the Podcast:** Briefly mention the podcast's name and purpose.
- **Set the Tone:** Use background music or sound effects that match your theme.
- **Example Intro:** "Welcome to *Startup Stories,* the podcast where we uncover the untold journeys of entrepreneurs. Let's dive into today's story!"

2. **Podcast Outro**

    - **Summarize the Episode:** Briefly recap what was discussed.
    - **Call to Action (CTA):** Encourage listeners to subscribe, leave a review, or visit your website.
    - **End on a Memorable Note:** Use a tagline, sound effect, or sign-off phrase. Example: "Thanks for tuning in to *Startup Stories.* Keep dreaming big, and we'll see you next time."

The Launch Strategy

Launching your podcast effectively is about more than just publishing your first episode. It's about building anticipation, attracting listeners, and creating momentum that keeps them coming back for more.

Recording and Releasing Multiple Episodes at Launch

1. **Why Launch with Multiple Episodes?**
    - **Increase Listener Engagement:** By providing more content upfront, you give listeners a reason to binge your episodes and subscribe.
    - **Showcase Variety:** Multiple episodes demonstrate the range of topics or styles your podcast will cover.
    - **Boost Algorithm Rankings:** Platforms like Apple Podcasts favor podcasts with high initial downloads and engagement.

2. **How Many Episodes to Launch With?**
    - Aim for at least 3-5 episodes at launch. This allows new listeners to sample different aspects of your podcast and get a feel for your style.

3. **Pre-Launch Preparation:**
    - **Batch Recording:** Record, edit, and finalize your launch episodes well in advance.
    - **Quality Over Quantity:** Focus on delivering polished content that represents your best work.

Timing Your Launch for Maximum Impact

1. **Choose the Right Day and Time:**
    - Research your target audience's listening habits. For instance, podcasts aimed at

commuters might perform better if released early in the morning.

- Many podcasters recommend launching on a Tuesday or Wednesday, as these are peak days for podcast downloads.

2. **Plan Around Key Dates:**
    - Avoid major holidays or events that might distract your audience.
    - Consider timing your launch to coincide with relevant trends or seasons. For example, a fitness podcast could launch in January to align with New Year's resolutions.

3. **Set Realistic Goals:**
    - Define what success looks like for your launch. Is it a specific number of downloads, social media followers, or email subscribers?

Generating Buzz Before Release

1. **Build Anticipation:**
    - **Teasers:** Share teaser clips, behind-the-scenes content, or countdown posts on social media.
    - **Website or Landing Page:** Create a simple website with details about your podcast, a mailing list signup, and links to your episodes.

2. **Leverage Your Network:**

- **Friends and Family:** Ask your personal network to listen, subscribe, and leave reviews.
- **Professional Contacts:** Reach out to colleagues or industry peers who might be interested in sharing your podcast.

3. **Collaborate with Influencers:**
   - Partner with influencers, bloggers, or fellow podcasters who align with your niche. Offer to exchange promotions or appear as a guest on their platforms.

4. **Engage on Social Media:**
   - Create profiles on platforms where your target audience is most active (e.g., Instagram, Twitter, LinkedIn).
   - Use hashtags, polls, and interactive posts to spark engagement.

5. **Run a Giveaway or Contest:**
   - Offer prizes like exclusive content, merchandise, or gift cards to encourage listeners to subscribe and share your podcast.

Step-by-Step Launch Checklist

1. **Finalize Your Episodes:**
   - Ensure all launch episodes are edited, polished, and ready for publishing.

2. **Set Up Hosting and Distribution:**
   - Choose a podcast hosting platform and submit your RSS feed to directories like Apple Podcasts, Spotify, and Google Podcasts.

3. **Promote Your Podcast:**
   - Schedule social media posts, email campaigns, and collaborations leading up to the launch.

4. **Monitor Analytics:**
   - Track downloads, subscriptions, and listener feedback to evaluate your launch's success.

5. **Celebrate and Adjust:**
   - Celebrate your launch day with your audience and use their feedback to refine future episodes.

Final Thoughts

Branding and launching your podcast effectively sets the stage for long-term success. By creating a strong identity, crafting engaging intros and outros, and executing a strategic launch plan, you'll attract an audience that's excited to tune in week after week. Remember, the effort you invest now will pay off as your podcast grows and connects with listeners around the world.

Chapter 7: Marketing Your Podcast

Once your podcast is launched, the work doesn't stop there. Marketing your podcast effectively is essential to growing your audience and ensuring long-term success. This chapter explores the best strategies for leveraging social media, building an email list, collaborating with others, and pitching your podcast to guests and the media.

Leveraging Social Media

Social media is one of the most powerful tools for promoting your podcast. It allows you to connect with your audience, share your content, and create buzz around your show. To succeed, focus on the platforms where your target audience is most active.

Platforms to Focus On for Podcast Promotion

1. **Instagram**
    - Ideal for creating visually appealing content and connecting with a younger audience.
    - Use Instagram Stories and Reels to share bite-sized clips and behind-the-scenes content.
    - Engage with followers through polls, Q&A sessions, and interactive posts.

2. **Twitter**
    - Great for sharing updates, joining trending conversations, and interacting with your audience in real time.

- Use hashtags related to your niche to increase visibility.
- Share links to new episodes, quotes from your podcast, and retweet listener feedback.

3. **Facebook**
   - Build a community by creating a dedicated Facebook group for your podcast.
   - Post updates, share relevant articles, and engage with members through live streams or discussion threads.

4. **TikTok**
   - Perfect for short, creative content that captures attention quickly.
   - Share highlights, funny moments, or teaser clips from your podcast.

5. **LinkedIn**
   - Best for podcasts targeting professionals or business audiences.
   - Share episodes that offer industry insights or career advice.
   - Connect with potential guests or collaborators in your niche.

6. **YouTube**
   - Upload full episodes or shorter clips for additional reach.

- Use eye-catching thumbnails and descriptive titles to attract viewers.
- Leverage YouTube's SEO features by adding keywords and tags.

Tips for Creating Engaging Posts

1. **Video Clips**
   - Create 30- to 60-second clips highlighting the most compelling moments of your episodes.
   - Add subtitles to make your videos accessible and engaging.

2. **Quotes and Snippets**
   - Share impactful quotes from your podcast as standalone graphics.
   - Use tools like Canva to design visually appealing posts.

3. **Behind-the-Scenes Content**
   - Show your audience what goes into making your podcast. Share photos or videos of your recording setup, editing process, or team.

4. **Call-to-Actions (CTAs)**
   - Encourage your followers to listen, subscribe, or leave a review by including clear CTAs in your posts.

5. **Hashtag Strategy**

- Use popular and niche hashtags to increase visibility. For example, #PodcastLife, #TrueCrimePodcast, or #FitnessTalk.

Building an Email List

An email list is a direct line to your audience and an invaluable tool for keeping them engaged with your podcast. Unlike social media, email allows you to communicate with your subscribers without relying on algorithms.

Encouraging Subscribers Through Exclusive Content and Updates

1. **Offer Value:**
   - Provide exclusive content, such as bonus episodes, behind-the-scenes insights, or early access to new episodes, as an incentive for signing up.
   - Example: "Join our mailing list and get a free guide to mastering time management, plus exclusive podcast content!"

2. **Send Regular Updates:**
   - Keep your subscribers informed about new episodes, upcoming guests, or special events.
   - Include personal messages or reflections to create a stronger connection.

3. **Create a Lead Magnet:**

- Develop a free resource that aligns with your podcast's theme. For example, a travel podcast might offer a downloadable packing checklist.

4. **Promote Your Email List:**
    - Mention your email list in your podcast episodes and social media posts.
    - Add a signup form to your website or landing page.

5. **Segment Your Audience:**
    - Group your subscribers based on their interests or engagement levels to send more targeted emails.

Collaborating and Networking

Collaboration and networking are essential for expanding your reach and establishing credibility in the podcasting world. By partnering with others, you can tap into new audiences and build mutually beneficial relationships.

Reaching Out to Other Podcasters for Cross-Promotion

1. **Identify Complementary Podcasts:**
    - Look for podcasts in your niche or with similar target audiences.
    - Reach out to podcasters whose content aligns with yours but doesn't directly compete.

2. **Propose Cross-Promotion:**
   - Exchange shoutouts or recommend each other's podcasts in your episodes.
   - Collaborate on joint episodes or interviews.
3. **Share Resources:**
   - Exchange tips, tools, or advice with fellow podcasters to build a supportive community.

Joining Podcasting Communities and Events

1. **Online Communities:**
   - Join Facebook groups, Reddit threads, or Discord servers dedicated to podcasting.
   - Participate in discussions, ask questions, and share your expertise.
2. **Podcasting Conferences and Meetups:**
   - Attend events like Podcast Movement or Podfest to network with industry professionals and learn from experts.
   - Use these opportunities to pitch your podcast, connect with potential guests, or find sponsors.
3. **Collaborate Locally:**
   - Connect with local podcasters or businesses for joint promotions or events.

Pitching to Guests and Media

Inviting interesting guests and gaining media coverage can significantly boost your podcast's visibility and credibility. Here's how to approach both effectively.

How to Invite Interesting Guests to Your Show

1. **Research Potential Guests:**
   - Identify individuals who are knowledgeable in your niche or have a unique story to tell.
   - Examples include authors, industry experts, influencers, or inspiring everyday people.

2. **Craft a Compelling Pitch:**
   - Personalize your invitation by mentioning why you admire their work and how their expertise aligns with your podcast.
   - Example: "Hi [Name], I'm a big fan of your work on [Project/Book]. I host a podcast called [Podcast Name], where we explore [Theme]. I'd love to feature you as a guest to discuss [Specific Topic]."

3. **Highlight the Benefits:**
   - Emphasize what's in it for them, such as exposure to your audience or an opportunity to promote their latest project.

4. **Make It Easy:**
   - Provide details about the recording process, time commitment, and any preparation required.

- Offer to accommodate their schedule as much as possible.

Writing Press Releases to Gain Media Coverage

1. **Identify Relevant Media Outlets:**
    - Research blogs, magazines, or websites that cover your podcast's niche.
    - Look for journalists or editors who write about podcasts or related topics.

2. **Craft a Newsworthy Angle:**
    - Highlight what makes your podcast unique, timely, or relevant to their audience.
    - Example: "Local Entrepreneur Launches Podcast to Empower Small Business Owners."

3. **Structure Your Press Release:**
    - **Headline:** Write a catchy and concise headline that grabs attention.
    - **Introduction:** Summarize the key details, including your podcast's name, purpose, and unique angle.
    - **Body:** Provide additional information, such as notable guests, launch details, or your personal story.
    - **Contact Information:** Include your name, email, and website for follow-ups.

4. **Distribute Your Press Release:**

- Send your press release via email to targeted journalists and bloggers.
- Use services like PRWeb or Presswire for wider distribution.

5. **Follow Up:**
   - Reach out politely a week after sending your press release to ensure it was received.

Final Thoughts

Marketing your podcast requires a combination of creativity, persistence, and strategic planning. By leveraging social media, building an email list, collaborating with others, and pitching effectively, you can grow your audience and establish your podcast as a must-listen. Remember, the key to successful marketing is building genuine connections with your listeners and the wider podcasting community.

Chapter 8: Monetizing Your Podcast

Monetizing your podcast can be a rewarding way to turn your passion project into a source of income. However, successful monetization requires timing, strategy, and maintaining the trust of your audience. This chapter explores when to start monetizing, various methods to generate revenue, and how to strike the right balance between earning income and staying authentic.

When to Start Monetizing

One of the most common questions for podcasters is when to start monetizing. While there's no one-size-fits-all answer, timing plays a crucial role in maximizing your income potential.

Knowing When Your Audience Size Is Ready

1. **Understand Industry Benchmarks**
    - Podcast sponsors often look for shows with a consistent listener base. A common benchmark for sponsorships is 500 to 1,000 downloads per episode within the first 30 days of release.
    - If your podcast has a smaller but highly engaged audience, you might still attract niche sponsors or explore alternative monetization methods.
2. **Focus on Engagement, Not Just Numbers**

- Sponsors value audience engagement just as much as download numbers. Metrics like listener retention, social media interactions, and email subscribers can demonstrate your podcast's influence.
- Build a loyal audience before monetizing. A small, dedicated following can lead to better long-term monetization opportunities than a large but disengaged listener base.

3. **Consistency Is Key**

    - Sponsors and premium subscribers look for reliable content creators. Ensure you have a regular posting schedule and high-quality episodes before pursuing monetization.
    - Consider waiting until you've released 10-15 episodes to establish your podcast's reputation.

4. **Test the Waters Early**

    - Experiment with small-scale monetization strategies, like affiliate marketing or selling merchandise, to gauge your audience's willingness to support your podcast financially.

Monetization Methods

There are many ways to monetize a podcast, from traditional sponsorships to creative approaches like offering exclusive content. Choosing the right method depends on your audience size, niche, and long-term goals.

Sponsorships and Ads

Sponsorships and ads are among the most common ways podcasters generate income.

1. **Types of Sponsorships**
    - **Pre-Roll Ads:** Short ads (15-30 seconds) played at the beginning of an episode.
    - **Mid-Roll Ads:** Longer ads (30-60 seconds) placed in the middle of an episode. These typically command higher rates due to their placement.
    - **Post-Roll Ads:** Ads placed at the end of an episode, often used for lower-stakes promotions.

2. **How to Attract Sponsors**
    - **Create a Media Kit:** Include key stats like download numbers, audience demographics, and engagement metrics. Highlight your podcast's unique value proposition.
    - **Pitch to Relevant Brands:** Identify companies that align with your audience's interests. For example, a fitness podcast might target health supplement brands.
    - **Join Podcast Ad Networks:** Platforms like Podcorn, AdvertiseCast, and Midroll connect podcasters with potential sponsors.

3. **Setting Ad Rates**
    - Podcast ads are often priced using CPM (cost per mille), which is the cost per 1,000

impressions. Typical rates range from $18 to $50 CPM, depending on your niche and engagement.
- Example: If you charge $25 CPM and average 2,000 downloads per episode, you can earn $50 per ad spot.

4. **Tips for Effective Ad Integration**
    - Keep ads relevant to your audience to maintain authenticity.
    - Use dynamic ad insertion to tailor ads based on listener demographics or location.
    - Share personal experiences with the product or service to make the ad feel genuine.

Creating Premium Content

Offering exclusive content is a popular way to monetize your podcast while rewarding loyal listeners.

1. **Platforms for Premium Content**
    - **Patreon:** Create a membership program where subscribers gain access to bonus episodes, early releases, or behind-the-scenes content.
    - **Supercast and Glow.fm:** Platforms designed specifically for podcast creators to offer premium subscriptions.
    - **Apple Podcasts Subscriptions and Spotify Paid Subscriptions:** Enable in-app subscriptions for ad-free episodes or bonus content.

2. **Ideas for Premium Content**
    - **Exclusive Episodes:** Share deeper dives into topics, Q&A sessions, or mini-series available only to subscribers.
    - **Ad-Free Listening:** Offer episodes without sponsorship interruptions.
    - **Early Access:** Release episodes to premium subscribers before the general public.
    - **Interactive Perks:** Host live Q&A sessions, virtual meetups, or personalized shoutouts.

3. **Pricing Premium Content**
    - Start with affordable tiers, such as $5 or $10 per month, and offer higher-priced tiers with additional perks.
    - Provide a clear value proposition for each tier to encourage upgrades.

Selling Your Own Products or Services

Monetizing through your own products or services gives you full control over your income and strengthens your brand.

1. **Merchandise**
    - Sell branded items like T-shirts, mugs, or stickers. Use platforms like Printful or Teespring for print-on-demand services.
    - Design merchandise that resonates with your audience. For example, include catchphrases or iconic imagery from your podcast.

2. **Courses and Workshops**
   - Leverage your expertise to create online courses or host workshops related to your podcast's niche.
   - Example: A finance podcast might offer a budgeting course, while a cooking podcast could host a virtual cooking class.

3. **Ebooks and Guides**
   - Compile insights, tips, or strategies from your podcast into an ebook or guide. Sell it directly through your website or platforms like Gumroad.

4. **Consulting or Coaching**
   - Position yourself as an authority in your field by offering one-on-one consulting or coaching services.
   - Example: A marketing podcaster could provide personalized strategies for small businesses.

5. **Affiliate Marketing**
   - Promote products or services relevant to your audience and earn a commission for each sale. Join affiliate programs like Amazon Associates or ShareASale.
   - Ensure transparency by disclosing affiliate links to maintain trust.

Balancing Monetization with Authenticity

While monetization is an exciting milestone, it's important to prioritize your audience's trust and ensure your podcast's content remains authentic.

Keeping Your Audience's Trust

1. **Be Transparent About Monetization**
    - Clearly disclose when you include sponsored content, ads, or affiliate links.
    - Example: "This episode is sponsored by [Brand]. As always, we only partner with companies we believe in."

2. **Choose Relevant Sponsors**
    - Partner with brands that align with your podcast's niche and values. Irrelevant or controversial sponsors can alienate your audience.
    - Example: A wellness podcast might partner with a meditation app but avoid fast-food chains.

3. **Maintain Content Quality**
    - Avoid overloading episodes with ads or promotions. Keep the focus on delivering valuable content.
    - Balance ad placement to ensure they don't disrupt the flow of your episodes.

Earning Income Without Compromising Authenticity

1. **Engage Your Audience in Monetization Decisions**
    - Involve your listeners by asking for feedback on premium content ideas or merchandise designs.
    - Example: "What perks would you like to see in our Patreon membership?"

2. **Deliver Value Before Asking for Support**
    - Build goodwill by consistently providing high-quality, free content. This fosters loyalty and encourages listeners to support your monetization efforts.

3. **Stay True to Your Mission**
    - Ensure that all monetization efforts align with your podcast's purpose and goals. Avoid ventures that feel out of place or purely profit-driven.

4. **Monitor Listener Feedback**
    - Pay attention to reviews, comments, and social media interactions to gauge how your audience responds to monetization efforts.
    - Adjust your strategy based on constructive criticism or trends.

Final Thoughts

Monetizing your podcast can open up exciting opportunities, but it requires thoughtful planning and a commitment to maintaining authenticity. Whether through sponsorships, premium content, or selling your own products, choose methods that align with your audience's needs and your podcast's values. By balancing monetization with genuine engagement, you can turn your podcast into a sustainable venture that benefits both you and your listeners.

Chapter 9: Measuring Success and Growing Your Podcast

Creating a podcast is a rewarding journey, but to ensure its long-term success, you need to measure its performance and continually work on audience growth. Understanding your metrics, retaining and expanding your audience, and evolving your content based on feedback are critical steps in maintaining and scaling your podcast.

Tracking Your Metrics

Measuring your podcast's success starts with understanding the key metrics that reveal how your content is performing and how your audience is engaging with it.

Analyzing Download Numbers

1. **What Download Numbers Tell You**
    - Download numbers are the most common metric for assessing a podcast's popularity.
    - Each download represents a listener accessing your content, though it doesn't guarantee full episode completion.

2. **Key Metrics to Monitor**
    - **Total Downloads:** The cumulative number of downloads for your podcast.
    - **Downloads per Episode:** Tracks the average downloads each episode receives. This is particularly useful for spotting trends in audience growth.

- **Download Timeframes:** Pay attention to downloads in the first 7-30 days after an episode's release, as these often reflect the most active listeners.

3. **Tools for Tracking Downloads**

    - Use podcast hosting platforms like Buzzsprout, Libsyn, or Anchor, which provide detailed analytics.
    - Platforms like Podtrac and Chartable offer additional insights into download performance and rankings.

Understanding Listener Demographics

1. **Demographic Insights**

    - Most hosting platforms provide data on listener demographics, including age, gender, location, and preferred listening devices.
    - Knowing your audience helps you tailor your content, marketing, and partnerships to their preferences.

2. **Why Demographics Matter**

    - Advertisers often base sponsorship decisions on audience demographics.
    - Demographics guide decisions on content topics, episode length, and promotional strategies.

Engagement Metrics

1. **Listener Retention**
    - Platforms like Spotify and Apple Podcasts offer insights into how long listeners stay engaged during an episode.
    - Monitor where listeners drop off to identify areas for improvement.
2. **Social Media and Website Analytics**
    - Track how your audience interacts with your content outside the podcast. Metrics like shares, likes, and comments can indicate engagement.
3. **Reviews and Ratings**
    - Listener reviews on platforms like Apple Podcasts provide qualitative feedback that reflects audience sentiment and loyalty.

Growing Your Audience

To ensure your podcast reaches new listeners and retains existing ones, focus on strategies for growth and engagement.

Strategies for Audience Retention and Referral

1. **Deliver Consistent Quality**
    - Regularly release high-quality episodes on a consistent schedule to build listener trust and anticipation.
2. **Engage with Your Audience**

- Interact with listeners on social media and through email to foster a sense of community.
- Respond to comments, questions, and feedback to show that you value their input.

3. **Encourage Word-of-Mouth Referrals**
    - Ask loyal listeners to share your podcast with friends and family.
    - Offer incentives like shoutouts, exclusive content, or giveaways for referrals.

4. **Create Shareable Content**
    - Produce bite-sized, shareable snippets of your podcast episodes for social media.
    - Include captions and graphics to make posts visually appealing and accessible.

Expanding into New Platforms

1. **Leverage YouTube**
    - Upload full episodes or shorter clips to YouTube to reach a broader audience. Use engaging thumbnails and SEO-friendly titles.
    - Consider creating video content alongside your audio episodes for increased visibility.

2. **Start a Blog**

- Repurpose podcast episodes into blog posts or articles to attract readers who may become listeners.
- Optimize your blog for search engines to increase organic traffic.

3. **Explore Live Shows and Events**
    - Host live podcast recordings or Q&A sessions on platforms like Instagram Live, Facebook Live, or Zoom.
    - Attend podcasting or industry-related events to network and showcase your podcast.

4. **Collaborate with Other Creators**
    - Appear as a guest on other podcasts or invite guests from related niches to cross-promote your content.

Developing a Long-Term Growth Strategy

1. **Track and Adjust**
    - Regularly review your analytics to identify trends and areas for improvement.
    - Adapt your growth strategy based on what's working and what's not.

2. **Invest in Paid Promotion**
    - Experiment with targeted ads on platforms like Facebook, Instagram, and Google to reach potential listeners.

- Collaborate with influencers or bloggers in your niche to expand your reach.

Adapting and Evolving

Podcasting is a dynamic medium that requires ongoing adaptation to stay relevant and engaging. Listening to feedback and refreshing your content can keep your audience interested and attract new listeners.

Gathering Feedback from Your Listeners

1. **Encourage Listener Feedback**
   - Regularly ask for feedback during episodes and on social media.
   - Use polls, surveys, or email forms to collect listener opinions.

2. **Monitor Reviews and Comments**
   - Pay attention to reviews on podcast directories and comments on social media for insights into what your audience loves and where they see room for improvement.

3. **Conduct Audience Surveys**
   - Create detailed surveys to learn more about your audience's preferences, challenges, and interests.
   - Offer incentives, like exclusive content, for survey participation.

Refreshing Your Format or Content Over Time

1. **Experiment with New Formats**
    - Introduce new segments, episode lengths, or styles to keep your content fresh.
    - For example, a storytelling podcast could add occasional interviews or panel discussions.
2. **Revisit Your Niche**
    - As your podcast evolves, your niche may need to expand or pivot. Stay attuned to industry trends and audience interests.
    - Example: A tech podcast could evolve from general topics to focus on emerging technologies like AI or blockchain.
3. **Seasonal Themes or Special Series**
    - Create limited-run series or themed seasons to explore topics in greater depth.
    - Announce themes in advance to build excitement and anticipation.
4. **Repackage Existing Content**
    - Revisit popular episodes to create updated versions or compilations.
    - Use evergreen content to attract new listeners while maintaining relevance.

Staying Ahead of Trends

1. **Monitor Industry Trends**

- Stay informed about changes in podcasting technology, listener habits, and market opportunities.
- Join podcasting communities or attend industry events to keep up with trends.

2. **Embrace New Platforms and Technologies**
   - Experiment with new platforms or tools that enhance the listener experience, such as interactive content or personalized recommendations.

3. **Keep Learning**
   - Continuously improve your skills by taking courses or attending workshops on storytelling, editing, or marketing.

Final Thoughts

Measuring your podcast's success and growing your audience is an ongoing process that requires careful analysis, creativity, and adaptability. By tracking your metrics, retaining your current audience, and expanding into new platforms, you can build a podcast that thrives over time. Remember, staying open to feedback and evolving your content ensures your podcast remains fresh, relevant, and engaging for your listeners.

Chapter 10: Overcoming Challenges in Podcasting

Podcasting is an incredibly rewarding journey, but it's not without its challenges. From creative blocks to managing negative feedback and maintaining consistency, every podcaster faces obstacles. This chapter explores common challenges, provides strategies for overcoming them, and offers practical tips for staying consistent in your podcasting efforts.

Common Obstacles

Every podcaster encounters hurdles that test their resolve and creativity. Understanding these challenges and knowing how to address them can make the journey smoother and more enjoyable.

Handling Creative Blocks or Burnout

1. **Recognizing the Signs**
    - Creative blocks often manifest as difficulty generating ideas, feeling uninspired, or lacking enthusiasm for recording.
    - Burnout includes symptoms like exhaustion, frustration, and a diminished sense of accomplishment.

2. **Strategies to Overcome Creative Blocks**
    - **Take a Break:** Stepping away from podcasting for a few days or weeks can help recharge your creativity.

- Seek Inspiration: Listen to other podcasts, read books, or watch videos in your niche to spark new ideas.
- Brainstorm with Others: Collaborate with friends, co-hosts, or fellow podcasters to generate fresh content ideas.
- Change Your Environment: Recording in a new location or working in a different setting can help you see things from a new perspective.
- Experiment with Formats: Try a new episode style, such as interviews, Q&A sessions, or storytelling, to reignite your passion.

3. Preventing Burnout

- Set Realistic Goals: Avoid overcommitting by planning a manageable schedule.
- Celebrate Milestones: Recognize and reward yourself for reaching achievements like publishing 10 episodes or growing your listener base.
- Prioritize Self-Care: Get adequate rest, exercise, and maintain a work-life balance to avoid exhaustion.
- Delegate Tasks: If possible, outsource editing, social media management, or other time-consuming tasks.

Dealing with Negative Feedback

1. **Understanding Criticism**
   - Negative feedback is a natural part of creating content. While it can sting, it often provides valuable insights into areas for improvement.

2. **How to Handle Criticism Gracefully**
   - **Separate Constructive Feedback from Trolls:** Focus on comments that offer specific suggestions or valid critiques. Ignore unhelpful or malicious remarks.
   - **Respond Professionally:** Thank listeners for their input, even if it's critical. Example: "Thank you for your feedback. I'll consider this as I plan future episodes."
   - **Avoid Arguing:** Responding defensively to negative comments can harm your reputation. Instead, approach criticism with an open mind.

3. **Using Feedback to Improve**
   - Regularly review listener comments, ratings, and reviews for patterns or recurring themes.
   - Use feedback to adjust content, improve audio quality, or refine your delivery style.

4. **Maintaining Perspective**
   - Remember that you can't please everyone. Focus on serving your target audience and staying true to your podcast's mission.

- Seek support from peers or podcasting communities to navigate challenging feedback.

Staying Consistent

Consistency is one of the most critical factors in building a successful podcast. A regular posting schedule fosters listener trust and helps grow your audience.

Building Habits to Maintain a Regular Posting Schedule

1. **Create a Content Calendar**
   - Plan your episodes several weeks or months in advance to stay organized.
   - Use tools like Google Calendar, Notion, or Trello to schedule topics, guest appearances, and deadlines.

2. **Set Realistic Expectations**
   - Choose a posting frequency that aligns with your availability and resources. Whether it's weekly, biweekly, or monthly, consistency matters more than frequency.

3. **Establish a Routine**
   - Dedicate specific days and times to podcast-related tasks, such as scripting, recording, and editing.
   - Treat podcasting like a job by committing to your schedule and minimizing distractions.

4. **Track Your Progress**
    - Monitor your adherence to the schedule and celebrate small victories, like meeting your deadlines or maintaining consistency for several months.

Tips for Batching Content and Staying Ahead of Deadlines

1. **What Is Content Batching?**
    - Content batching involves completing multiple tasks in one sitting to maximize efficiency. For example, recording several episodes in one day or editing a batch of audio files at once.

2. **Benefits of Content Batching**
    - Saves time by reducing context switching.
    - Provides a buffer of prepared episodes, reducing stress if unexpected events arise.
    - Allows you to focus on other podcasting tasks, like marketing and engagement.

3. **How to Batch Content Effectively**
    - **Plan in Advance:** Outline multiple episodes at once to streamline scripting and recording.
    - **Set Dedicated Days:** Allocate specific days for batching tasks, such as recording all morning and editing in the afternoon.

- **Streamline Your Workflow:** Use templates for show notes, intros, and outros to save time.
- **Prioritize High-Energy Tasks First:** Start with recording or brainstorming while your energy is at its peak.

4. **Avoid Common Pitfalls**
   - Don't sacrifice quality for quantity. Ensure each episode is well-researched and polished, even when batching.
   - Take breaks during long batching sessions to avoid burnout.

Staying Ahead of Deadlines

1. **Set Internal Deadlines**
   - Establish personal deadlines ahead of your actual release dates to account for unexpected delays.
   - Example: If your podcast goes live every Friday, aim to complete editing by Wednesday.

2. **Use Automation Tools**
   - Schedule episode uploads, social media posts, and email campaigns using tools like Hootsuite, Buffer, or your podcast hosting platform.

3. **Build a Buffer**

- Maintain a backlog of 2-3 completed episodes to ensure you can release content even during busy weeks or unforeseen circumstances.

4. **Outsource When Needed**
    - Delegate tasks like editing, transcription, or graphic design to freelancers or virtual assistants. Platforms like Fiverr or Upwork can connect you with skilled professionals.

Final Thoughts

Overcoming challenges in podcasting requires resilience, adaptability, and a proactive approach. By addressing creative blocks, handling criticism constructively, and staying consistent in your efforts, you'll be well-equipped to navigate the ups and downs of podcasting. Remember, every obstacle is an opportunity to grow, refine your skills, and strengthen your podcast's foundation for long-term success.

Conclusion: Your Podcasting Journey

Podcasting is an exciting, ever-evolving platform for sharing ideas, stories, and expertise. Whether you're just starting or refining your craft, the journey is one of growth, creativity, and connection. In this conclusion, we'll focus on encouraging you to take that first step, embrace imperfection, and explore the promising future of podcasting.

Encouragement to Start Now

Starting a podcast can feel daunting. You may worry about whether your voice is compelling enough, if your equipment is adequate, or if anyone will even listen. These fears are common but not insurmountable. The most successful podcasters began with a simple decision: to start.

Overcoming the Fear of Imperfection

1. **Perfection Is the Enemy of Progress**
    - Many aspiring podcasters delay launching because they want everything to be perfect. However, waiting for perfection often leads to stagnation.
    - Remember, podcasting is a learning process. Your first episode won't be flawless, and that's okay. Every recording is an opportunity to improve.
2. **Embrace Authenticity**

- Listeners are drawn to genuine voices and relatable stories. Authenticity often resonates more than polished production.
- Example: Some of the most popular podcasts started with minimal equipment and a simple format. Over time, they evolved into professional productions.

3. **Redefine Success**
   - Success isn't just about download numbers or sponsorships. It's about creating something meaningful, connecting with your audience, and sharing your passion.
   - Set personal goals that focus on progress, like producing a set number of episodes or improving your editing skills.

4. **Learn as You Go**
   - Don't wait until you've mastered every aspect of podcasting to begin. Start with what you know and adapt along the way.
   - Resources like online tutorials, podcasting communities, and books can help you refine your craft over time.

Taking the First Step with Confidence

1. **Start Small and Simple**
   - Begin with a basic setup and focus on delivering valuable content. You don't need a professional studio or expensive equipment to get started.

- Example: Record your first episode using a USB microphone and free editing software like Audacity or GarageBand.

2. **Set Realistic Goals**
   - Break your podcasting journey into manageable steps. Start with creating a concept, recording a pilot episode, and sharing it with a small group for feedback.
   - Celebrate each milestone, whether it's publishing your first episode or reaching 100 downloads.

3. **Leverage Your Network**
   - Share your podcast with friends, family, and colleagues who can provide support and constructive feedback.
   - Use your existing social media channels to promote your podcast and build a loyal listener base.

4. **Trust Your Voice**
   - Your perspective and experiences are unique. Trust that your voice matters and that there are people who will benefit from hearing your message.
   - Over time, you'll grow more confident in your abilities and find your distinctive style.

The Future of Podcasting

The podcasting landscape is rapidly evolving, offering exciting opportunities for creators. Staying informed about emerging trends and technologies can help you grow and adapt in this dynamic medium.

Trends to Watch

1. **The Rise of Niche Content**
    - As the number of podcasts increases, listeners are gravitating toward shows that cater to specific interests or communities.
    - Opportunity: Focus on a unique niche that aligns with your expertise or passion. Niche podcasts often have highly engaged audiences.

2. **Interactive and Immersive Experiences**
    - Advancements in technology are enabling more interactive podcasting formats, such as live Q&A sessions, audience polls, and immersive audio experiences.
    - Opportunity: Experiment with new formats or incorporate interactive elements to deepen audience engagement.

3. **Increased Monetization Options**
    - Platforms like Patreon, Supercast, and Apple Podcasts Subscriptions are making it easier for creators to monetize their content through memberships and exclusive offerings.

- Opportunity: Explore multiple revenue streams, from sponsorships to premium content, to sustain and grow your podcast.

4. **AI and Automation Tools**
    - AI-powered tools are simplifying podcast production, from editing to transcription and analytics.
    - Opportunity: Use tools like Descript or Adobe Podcast to streamline your workflow and focus more on content creation.

5. **Expansion of Podcast Networks**
    - Podcast networks are growing, providing creators with resources, cross-promotion opportunities, and access to larger audiences.
    - Opportunity: Consider joining a network or collaborating with other podcasters to amplify your reach.

Opportunities to Grow

1. **Global Reach**
    - With the rise of multilingual podcasts and translation tools, creators can reach audiences beyond their native language.
    - Opportunity: Expand your podcast's accessibility by offering translations or subtitles for key episodes.

2. **Collaborations and Partnerships**

- Collaborating with other podcasters, brands, or influencers can help you tap into new audiences and bring fresh perspectives to your show.
- Opportunity: Build relationships within your niche and seek mutually beneficial partnerships.

3. **Video Podcasting**
    - Platforms like YouTube and Spotify are embracing video podcasts, allowing creators to engage audiences visually.
    - Opportunity: Experiment with video formats to enhance your content and attract viewers who prefer visual media.

4. **Focus on Analytics**
    - Advanced analytics tools are offering deeper insights into listener behavior and preferences.
    - Opportunity: Use data to refine your content, target your marketing efforts, and improve audience retention.

5. **Diversity and Inclusion**
    - As podcasting becomes more mainstream, there's a growing demand for diverse voices and perspectives.
    - Opportunity: Share stories that represent underrepresented communities or unique viewpoints.

Adapting to Change

1. **Stay Informed**
   - Follow industry news, join podcasting forums, and attend conferences to stay ahead of trends.
   - Resources like Podcast Movement and PodNews provide valuable insights into the evolving landscape.

2. **Embrace Experimentation**
   - Don't be afraid to try new formats, topics, or technologies. Innovation often leads to growth and new opportunities.

3. **Focus on Your Audience**
   - Continuously engage with your listeners and adapt your content to meet their needs and preferences.
   - Regularly solicit feedback through surveys, social media, or direct communication.

Final Thoughts

Your podcasting journey is unique to you. It's a space where you can express yourself, connect with others, and make an impact. By starting now, embracing imperfection, and staying open to the future's possibilities, you're setting yourself up for success.

Remember, every great podcaster began with a single episode. The key is to take that first step, trust your voice, and keep moving forward. As the podcasting world continues to grow and evolve, so too will your opportunities to share your story and build something truly special. Your journey is just beginning—and the possibilities are endless.

www.ingramcontent.com/pod-product-compliance
Lightning Source LLC
Chambersburg PA
CBHW071105240526
45469CB00006BD/2339